MARCHING FOR CHANGE

MOVEMENTS ACROSS AMERICA

by Joyce Markovics

Throughout our country's history, millions of Americans have marched shoulder to shoulder and hand in hand for a common goal. The marchers—ordinary people from different backgrounds—protested injustice. They spoke out against powerful groups that unfairly treated those who were less powerful. These marchers fought for freedom and demanded change for themselves and others.

This book describes three important protest marches that shaped—and are still shaping—the history of the United States. You'll read about the 1963 March on Washington, the 2017 Women's March, and, finally, the Black Lives Matter marches that began in 2020.

Whether fighting for civil rights, equal pay, access to jobs, or calling for an end to racism and police brutality, these protest marches are united by one message—equality and justice for *all*.

Keep marching, America.

SLEEPING BEAR PRESS™
2395 South Huron Parkway, Suite 200
Ann Arbor, MI 48104
www.sleepingbearpress.com

Printed and bound in the United States.

10 9 8 7 6 5 4 3 2 1

Library of Congress Cataloging-in-Publication Data on file.

Reading Adviser: Marla Conn, MS Ed., Literacy specialist, Read-Ability, Inc. | Content Adviser: Emilye Crosby, PhD | Book Designer: Felicia Macheske

Graphics Credits: © Essl/Shutterstock; © majivecka/Shutterstock; © Margaret Jone Wollman/Shutterstock; © melitas/Shutterstock; © tandaV/Shutterstock

Photo Credits: Photograph by Marion S. Trikosko/Library of Congress, LOC Control No.: 2013648843, 5; Courtesy of U.S. Archives and Records Administration, 6, 8, 15, 16, 17,18, 19; Photograph by Carl van Vechten/Library of Congress, LOC Control No.: 2004663076, 7; Photograph by Warren K. Leffler/Library of Congress, LOC Control No.: 2011648314, 7; © user15783148/Freepik.com, 9; Photograph by Orlando Fernandex/Library of Congress, LOC Control No.: 2003671269, 9; Photograph by John Vachon/Library of Congress, LOC Control No.: 2017717044, 10; © Everett Collection/ Shutterstock, 11; Photograph by John Borgetta/Library of Congress, LOC Control No.: 97519529, 12; © JNix/Shutterstock, 12; Photograph by Warren K. Leffler/Library of Congress, LOC Control No.: 2016646651, 13; The Visibility Project/Wikimedia Commons, 13; Library of Congress, LOC Control No.: 97518862, 14; Marion S. Trikosko via Wikimedia Commons, 15; © Johnny Silvercloud/Shutterstock,, 21; Mobilus In Mobili/CC BY-SA 2.0/Wikimedia Commons, 21; © Julie Hassett Sutton/Shutterstock, 22; © B R O N, 23;/Shutterstock, 23; Wikimedia Commons, 24, 25, 30, 45; Photograph by F. Gutekunst/Library of Congress, 25; Photograph by Warren K. Leffler/Library of Congress, LOC Control No.: 2003673992, 26; Photograph by Fred Palumbo via Wikimedia Commons, 27; © Jamia Wilson, 29, 31; © Evan El-Amin/Shutterstock, 28; © Joseph Sohm/Shutterstock, 28; Photograph by Warren K. Leffler/Library of Congress, LOC Control No.: 2003654393, 29; © Yaacov Dagan/Alamy, 32;© Michael Candelori/Shutterstock,32; © StoopDown/Shutterstock, 33; © Tverdokhlib/Shutterstock, 35; Dan Aasland/CC BY-SA 2.0 via Wikimedia Commons, 35; © Julian Leshay/Shutterstock, 36; Photograph by Jack Delano/Library of Congress, LOC Control No.: 2017747598, 38; Photograph by Warren K. Leffler/Library of Congress, LOC Control No.: 2003688126, 39; © ESB Professional/Shutterstock, 39; © Skyward Kick Productions/Shutterstock, 40; © Ira Bostic/Shutterstock, 41; © a katz/Shutterstock, 42; © Rena Schild/Shutterstock, 42; © Associated Press, 42; FloNight/CC BY-SA 4.0/Wikimedia Commons, 43; Vasanth Rajkumar/CC BY-SA 4.0/Wikimedia Commons, 44; © hkalkan/Shutterstock, 45; © Michal Urbanek/Shutterstock, 46; © Eli Wilson/Shutterstock, 47

Table of Contents

1963 MARCH ON WASHINGTON

"We must say: 'Wake up America! Wake up!'

For we cannot stop, and we will not and cannot be patient."

—John Lewis
March on Washington speech, August 28, 1963

Coming Together

The morning of August 28, 1963, was warm and damp. Ericka Jenkins, a Black teenager, watched as a sea of people arrived in Washington, D.C. Some had traveled for days to reach her home city. "I've never been so awestruck," she said. "They came every way . . . buses, station wagons, cars, motorcycles, bicycles."

People from different backgrounds were pouring into Washington for an important reason. They were going to march for equal rights for Black Americans.

Buses arrive in Washington, D.C.

Jay Hardo, who was 82 years old, rode his bike from Dayton, Ohio, all the way to Washington, D.C. Another man, Ledger Smith, roller-skated 700 miles (1,127 kilometers) to get there!

By 9:00 a.m., around 40,000 people had gathered near the Washington Monument. They spread out blankets and sang songs about freedom. Ericka followed the crowds. She had never seen so many Black people in one place. And there were White people too. They were all going to march together.

"I saw people laughing and listening and standing very close to one another," Ericka said. "Their eyes were open, they were listening. I had never seen anything like that."

Famous musicians sang and played for the crowd. They included singers Mahalia Jackson, Odetta, and Bob Dylan.

Gospel singer Mahalia Jackson

The crowd continued to swell. By early afternoon, over 2,000 buses had dropped off more than 100,000 people. It was turning into the largest protest in U.S. history! Together, around 250,000 people—young and old, rich and poor—began to march to the Lincoln Memorial.

Thousands of people gathered at the Lincoln Memorial.

Within the Lincoln Memorial is a large statue of Abraham Lincoln. It honors the president who helped end slavery. That's where civil rights leaders, including Dr. Martin Luther King Jr., would speak and change the course of history.

The protest was also known as the March on Washington for Jobs and Freedom. At the time, Black people had fewer freedoms and less access to jobs.

Many marchers held signs or wore "March on Washington" buttons pinned to their clothing.

What Led to the March?

For hundreds of years, Black people were enslaved in America. Slavery ended in 1865 after the Civil War. But Black Americans still did not have equal rights. In the South, rules called Jim Crow laws kept them segregated.

Because of discriminatory laws, Black families could only buy homes in certain areas. These neighborhoods were usually run-down.

By law, Black people were not allowed to go to many of the same restaurants, hospitals, and schools as White people. Black schools often had fewer books and supplies. Also, Black people had to use separate water fountains and ride in the backs of the buses. If they broke these rules, they could be thrown in jail or even killed.

Black workers in the South

Living under Jim Crow laws was terrifying for Black people. However, there were Americans who stood up against racism. Asa Philip Randolph was a Black labor leader In the 1900s. He wanted better jobs and pay for Black workers.

In 1941, Randolph took on the U.S. government. He called for equal rights for Black defense workers. Randolph and other activists planned a march on Washington. When President Franklin D. Roosevelt finally agreed to help protect these workers, the march was called off. However, Randolph never forgot the idea. A big march could be a powerful tool for racial justice.

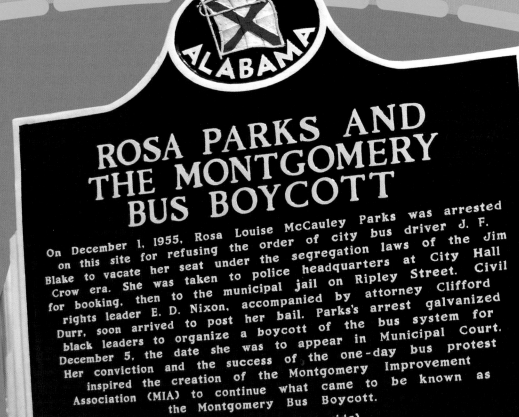

ROSA PARKS AND THE MONTGOMERY BUS BOYCOTT

On December 1, 1955, Rosa Louise McCauley Parks was arrested on this site for refusing the order of city bus driver J. F. Blake to vacate her seat under the segregation laws of the Jim Crow era. She was taken to police headquarters at City Hall for booking, then to the municipal jail on Ripley Street. Civil rights leader E. D. Nixon, accompanied by attorney Clifford Durr, soon arrived to post her bail. Parks's arrest galvanized black leaders to organize a boycott of the bus system for December 5, the date she was to appear in Municipal Court. Her conviction and the success of the one-day bus protest inspired the creation of the Montgomery Improvement Association (MIA) to continue what came to be known as the Montgomery Bus Boycott.

(Continued on other side)

2015

Martin Luther King, Jr.

Another strong leader was Dr. Martin Luther King Jr. He believed that Black people deserved the same rights as White people. In 1955, King was a young pastor in Montgomery, Alabama, when an event on a city bus changed his life. A Black woman named Rosa Parks refused to give up her bus seat to a White man. Afterward, she was arrested.

E. D. Nixon, an activist who worked with Randolph, helped start the "bus boycott." King eagerly joined him. During the protest, Black people stopped riding city buses in Montgomery. The 382-day protest led to a court decision that made segregation illegal. King rose to fame as a national civil rights leader.

Nine months before Rosa Parks's arrest, 15-year-old Claudette Colvin refused to give up her seat to a White woman on a Montgomery bus. "It's my constitutional right to sit here," she bravely said to the policemen removing her from the bus.

Claudette Colvin

"I Have A Dream"

In June 1963, after years of fighting for change, Randolph, King, and others planned a protest march on Washington. "Something dramatic must be done," said King. They asked Bayard Rustin, an activist and friend of Randolph's, to organize the event. He was gifted at planning. Rustin figured out all the details of the march in less than two months.

Bayard Rustin made sure marchers had everything they needed. This included food, bathrooms, and medical care!

The organizers had planned on 100,000 people attending the march. When 250,000 showed up from across the country, they were thrilled. Randolph spoke first. Others took the stage after him, delivering powerful speeches. Finally, Randolph introduced King.

Civil rights activist John Lewis was the youngest speaker.

John Lewis

King stepped up to the stage. The crowd cheered.
He spoke slowly and movingly. He talked of the need
for freedom, equality, and justice.

Now is the time to lift our nation from the quicksands of racial injustice to the solid rock of brotherhood. . . . I have a dream that one day . . . the sons of former slaves and the sons of former slave owners will be able to sit down together . . . I have a dream today!

Shouts of joy filled the mall. Randolph listened and wept. It was one of the greatest speeches—and greatest gatherings in support of Black Americans—in U.S. history.

People who couldn't attend the march watched the speeches on TV.

Action and Change

After years of protests and the march, the Civil Rights Act of 1964 was passed. It outlawed discrimination based on race and color. It also helped push schools to end segregation. Not long after, in 1965, the Voting Rights Act was passed. It stopped discrimination in voting.

"From every mountainside, let freedom ring!" King famously said on that warm August day. The March on Washington led to important changes, allowing freedom to ring more truly for Black Americans than it ever had. But more changes are still needed, and the march for freedom continues to this day.

The new law helped thousands more Black Americans vote.

2017 WOMEN'S MARCH

"We are linked.
We are not ranked.
And this is a day
that will change us
forever
because we are
together.
Each of us
individually and
collectively
will never be
the same again."

—Gloria Steinem
Women's March speech, January 21, 2017

Hand in Hand

A young girl stood smiling between her grandmother and mother. The three generations of females clasped hands. They were among the 5 million people who marched on January 21, 2017. They were united by a simple message: women's rights are human rights. "I'm not just doing it for myself . . . I'm doing it for my daughters and granddaughters," shouted a former teacher. People gathered in all 50 states. It was the biggest protest in U.S. history!

That day, people also marched for other issues that relate to women's rights. These included immigration, healthcare, and racial equality.

Of the millions of marchers, many were in Washington, D.C.

Around 500,000 people marched in Washington, D.C. They packed into a large park known as the National Mall. There was a sea of bright-pink hats. People wore them as a symbol of unity and women's rights.

To show their support, women who couldn't join the march knitted pink hats. Then they gave them to the marchers.

Marchers also carried colorful homemade signs. One read "Freedom." Another read "Girl Power!" The protesters sang and chanted "Equality for all" and "The future is female." They marched, side by side, as one big family.

WOMEN'S RIGHTS
ARE
HUMAN RIGHTS

I don't care for Trump

Rising Up

Throughout much of U.S. history, women were denied the same rights as men. In the early 1800s, for example, women could not own homes, work at the same jobs as men, or vote.

In 1848, women and their allies gathered in Seneca Falls, New York, to discuss women's rights. The planners created a document that demanded equality for women and the right to vote. Word soon spread around the country. Women began marching and holding rallies. Finally, in 1920, they won voting rights!

Lucretia Mott was one of the organizers of the Seneca Falls Convention.

The document was called the Declaration of Sentiments.

Even after winning the right to vote, women struggled to be treated fairly and with respect. In the 1960s and 1970s, women started calling for a greater role in society outside the home. They wanted the freedom to choose their own paths, careers, and families. These women called themselves feminists. "We're a movement now," yelled feminist Kate Millett to 50,000 marchers in New York in 1970. Author Betty Friedan led the march. It was known as the Women's Strike for Equality.

The Women's Strike for Equality took place 50 years after women won the right to vote. It celebrated the passing of the 19th Amendment.

In 1963, Betty Friedan wrote a book called *The Feminine Mystique*. It spoke of the need for women to be more than just wives and mothers.

Author and feminist Betty Friedan

Over the next 45 years, women had more choices than ever available to them. But the fight for equal rights is not over. In 2016, Donald Trump, a TV star and businessman, was elected president. He defeated Hillary Clinton, even though she had more government experience.

Hillary Clinton was the most successful female presidential candidate in American history.

Hillary Clinton

Trump's election and politics deeply angered many people. He spoke negatively about women—and even about violating them. Women and their allies wanted to take action. In response, they planned a march the day after Trump took office.

Donald Trump

The #MeToo movement came to light soon after Trump was elected. That's when many women began speaking out about being harassed by men in their workplaces.

#MeToo

The March

The Women's March took about 3 months to plan. The planners included activists from different races and backgrounds. Each had a unique point of view. As a team, they worked out the details of what would be a massive march. The event was taking shape. Excitement was growing.

Jamia Wilson, a Black woman and feminist, decided that she wanted to be a part of the march. "I come from a long line of activists who 'made a way out of no way,'" she said. Her family had marched for civil rights and to end segregation.

Jamia Wilson is a writer and feminist in New York City. She's the publisher of *The Feminist Press* at the City University of New York.

Civil rights activists in 1963

"Over the years, I've attended more marches than I can count," said Wilson. "But I knew this one was different when I encountered droves of pink-hatted women." The day of the Women's March, people flooded into Washington, D.C. There was an "endless stream of buses," she remembers.

Marchers assembling in Washington, D.C.

Jamia Wilson and filmmaker Alison Fast at the 2017 Women's March

"We stood together," Wilson said. "When people come together, share resources, and turn our daring discussions into opportunities to grow and change, there's nothing we can't do."

There were 653 separate marches that made up the 2017 Women's March. Organizers expected over 200,000 people to participate in Washington, D.C. Instead, 500,000 showed up!

Different speakers took the stage at the Women's March. They included famous actors and activists. One activist was Gloria Steinem. "Our constitution doesn't begin with 'I, the President,'" she said. "It begins with 'We, the People.'" She went on to say, "We are linked as human beings, not ranked by race or gender or class or any other label."

Gloria Steinem is a famous feminist activist.

Sophie Cruz, the youngest speaker that day, was only 6 years old. "Let us fight with love, faith, and courage," she proudly said. "There are still many people who have their hearts filled with love."

Sophie Cruz is a young Mexican American activist. She read her speech in both English and Spanish.

Time for Change

After the march, Hillary Clinton called it "awe-inspiring." Senator Bernie Sanders said Trump should "listen to the needs of women" as well as the needs of all Americans seeking equality. To keep people engaged, the march's organizers called for "10 Actions for the First 100 Days." This included a letter-writing campaign and phone calls to senators. The historic 2017 Women's March, with its powerful message of equality for all, uplifted and united people. One marcher said, "It changed my attitude. It also changed my action."

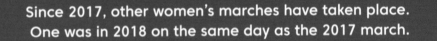

Since 2017, other women's marches have taken place. One was in 2018 on the same day as the 2017 march.

2020
BLACK LIVES MATTER MARCHES

"No more senseless killings of human beings. No more seeing people of color as less than human. We can no longer look away."

—Beyoncé
May 29, 2020

Justice Now!

"I can't breathe! I can't breathe!" protesters shouted over and over in the spring and summer of 2020. They marched as an army of thousands in 2,000 cities and towns across America. The Black, White, and brown protesters pumped their fists in unity. Their message was clear. Police brutality and racism must end. The marches were sparked after police choked and killed an unarmed Black man in March 2020. His name was George Floyd.

George Floyd is one of many Black Americans who have been killed by police.

Many of the protesters held homemade signs. A Black man carried a poster that said "Stop Killing Us." Another sign read "Black Lives Matter" in big, bold letters. Some people held up portraits of Floyd. A lot of protesters were marching for the first time ever.

"I was really, really surprised by the amount of people who turned out and how diverse the crowd was," said an Indian woman. A White man said he planned to attend as many marches as he could. "I plan on staying the course as long as it takes to achieve radical change."

A group called the Black Lives Matter Global Network inspired many of the protests.

Black Lives Matter

The shooting of George Floyd drew attention to the country's ongoing problem of racism. During the 1960s, Black Americans were not allowed to go to the same schools or hospitals as White people in parts of the country. They were denied access to vote and certain jobs. If they didn't follow the countless harsh rules set up by White people, they faced severe punishment. Thousands of activists and ordinary people fought for equal rights for Black Americans.

A 1940 photo showing a segregated bus station in North Carolina where Black people were kept apart from White people.

The efforts of civil rights leaders brought about new laws that helped protect Black people. But this did not stop structural racism throughout the country.

"We been waitin' all our lives, and still gettin' killed, still gettin' hung, still gettin' beat to death. Now we're tired waitin'!" said activist Fannie Lou Hamer in the 1960s.

Fannie Lou Hamer

In the recent past, the U.S. government made it harder for Black people to afford housing. This led to crowded slums.

Structural racism offers White people advantages that Black Americans cannot get. For example, it's more difficult for Black people to get a quality education, live in safe neighborhoods, access healthcare, and find good jobs. This occurs despite laws that protect them from discrimination.

As a result of structural racism, Black people are six times more likely than White people to be put in prison. Even more troubling, Black men are more than twice as likely to be shot and killed by police as White men.

Because of racism, Black men are viewed as more dangerous than other people. This can lead to false arrests and killings.

Protesters march for Trayvon Martin.

In February 2012, a Black teenager named Trayvon Martin was shot and killed on his way home from a store in Florida. The man who shot Martin thought the 17-year-old looked suspicious and dangerous. In his trial, the shooter was found not guilty.

This news saddened many Americans, including three female activists. For them and others, this decision meant that Martin's life and other Black lives didn't matter. To demand justice, they invented the phrase Black Lives Matter.

Two years later, in 2014, police killed a young, unarmed Black man named Michael Brown in Missouri. The policeman who shot Brown multiple times was not charged with a crime. Thousands marched—and kept marching—to protest the killing. This uprising turned Black Lives Matter into a movement.

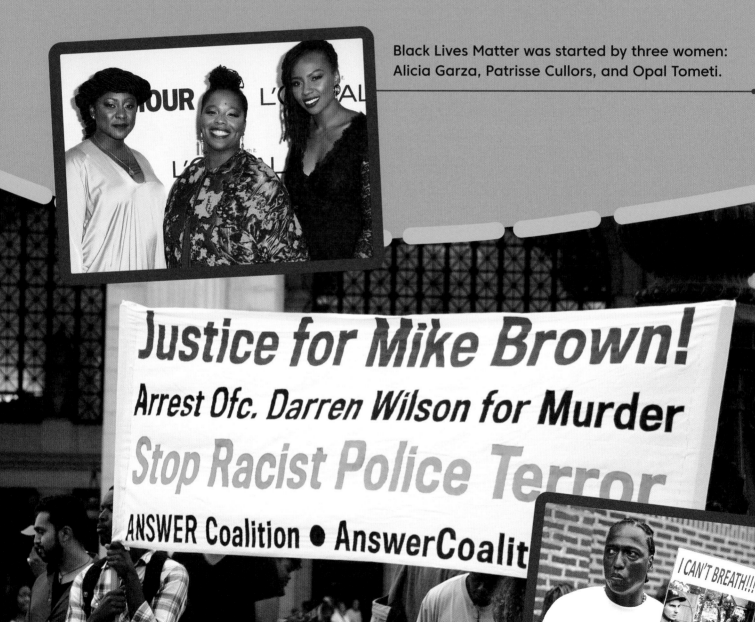

Black Lives Matter was started by three women: Alicia Garza, Patrisse Cullors, and Opal Tometi.

Justice for Mike Brown!
Arrest Ofc. Darren Wilson for Murder
Stop Racist Police Terror
ANSWER Coalition ● AnswerCoalit

I CAN'T BREATH!!!

I CAN'T BREATH!!!

RIP
Bro. Eric Garner

"Black Lives Matter" means that Black lives should be just as important as other lives.

That same year, more Black lives were lost. Eric Garner, a father and grandfather, was choked to death by New York police. Tamir Rice, a Black 12-year-old, was shot by a White cop in Ohio. Brown, Garner, and Rice are three of the dozens of Black people who have died at the hands of police in the past 20 years.

Breonna Taylor's memorial in Louisville, Kentucky, where she was shot.

The victims of police shootings also include women. Police shot Breonna Taylor eight times in her home in 2020.

The Marches

On May 25, 2020, a policeman in Minneapolis, Minnesota, forced George Floyd to the ground. He knelt on Floyd's neck for almost 9 minutes until Floyd stopped breathing. Before he died, Floyd cried out that he couldn't breathe. Onlookers, one of whom took a video of the incident, tried to help him. Yet the police refused to stop hurting Floyd.

This is where George Floyd lost his life. Teenager Darnella Frazier recorded his arrest and death on her phone.

The video of Floyd's killing spread around the country. It shocked and angered people. Hundreds of thousands of protesters took to the streets to demand justice for Floyd—and the other victims who came before him.

George Floyd

Most of marches were peaceful, but some turned violent. Unfortunately, the violent ones were shown more often in the news.

The protesters marched for something bigger as well. They wanted to stop violence against Black people. They also wanted to hold police who abuse their power accountable for their actions.

In addition, the Black Lives Matter marchers focused on the widespread problem of structural racism. They demanded that leaders listen. And they called on everybody in the country to take action to fight racism.

Protest marches are an important part of American history. They helped women earn the right to vote and workers get better pay.

A Call for Change

Soon after the marches began, small changes started happening. In Minneapolis, where George Floyd lost his life, the city started taking steps to rethink and reform the role of the police.

However, ending structural racism is a bigger fight. It involves changes to education, healthcare, housing, and jobs so that Black people have the same advantages as White people. "Protest is not the end of progress, it is the beginning. . . . I believe in us," said the musician Lizzo, urging people to keep up the fight.

Hundreds of different organizations fight for racial justice. These include Dream Defenders, BYP100, and Movement for Black Lives.

For Adam and all people who serve their communities and stand up for what is right.

—JM

JOYCE MARKOVICS lives in a very old house in historic Ossining, New York. As a child, she loved making art, reading, and writing stories. Today, she has authored more than 200 books for young readers. She believes that everybody should speak up and take an active role in protecting the rights of all people who are discriminated against. She believes in marching for change.

 Newham London

11/04/13		

24 hour automated telephone renewal line
0115 929 3388
Or online at www.newham.gov.uk

This book must be returned (or its issue renewed)
on or before the date stamped above

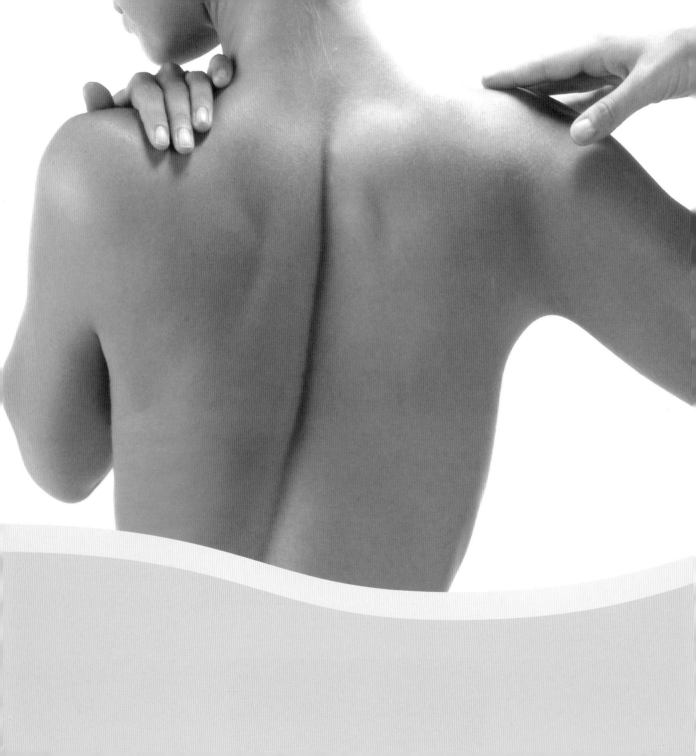